Greg Pembroke lives in Rochester, New York, with his wife and two young sons. He divides his time between working as a radio advertising copywriter, and looking after his sons at home. This is his first book.

REASONS MY KID IS CRYING

Greg Pembroke

BOXTREE

First published 2013 by Boxtree
an imprint of Pan Macmillan,
a division of Macmillan Publishers Limited
Pan Macmillan, 20 New Wharf Road, London N1 9RR
Basingstoke and Oxford
Associated companies throughout the world
www.panmacmillan.com

ISBN 978-1-4472-5268-9

9 8 7 6 5 4 3 2 1

A CIP catalogue record for this book is available from
the British Library.

Typeset/designed by ApeInc.co.uk
Printed by L.E.G.O. SpA Vicenza, Italy

Visit www.panmacmillan.com to read more about all our books and
to buy them. You will also find features, author interviews and news
of any author events, and you can sign up for e-newsletters so that
you're always first to hear about our new releases.

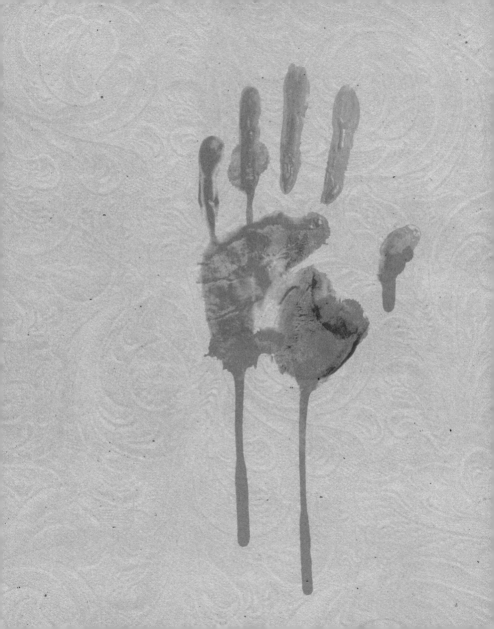

Send Attach

Reasons My Kid is Crying started when I posted a few pictures on Facebook of my three-year-old son, mid-tantrum, in an album called 'Reasons My Son is Crying'.

I had broken his cheese in half.

My friends loved it and encouraged me to start a blog so they could share the pictures with their friends as well. Within a few days of its creation, 'Reasons My Son Is Crying' had reached No.1 on the front page of Reddit, and was being shared so fast that Facebook's own spam filters began automatically blocking users from posting links to it. Within a week it had spread all over the world.

As people shared the blog and bonded over the universal human experience that is the toddler meltdown, a community was born – and the submissions started pouring in, many of which you will find in this book.

The most common type of email I received was that of thanks from parents around the globe who thought that their child was the only one who 'lost it' over the smallest of things. I'm happy to dispel this myth – and hope that this book will serve as a poignant reminder, for burned-out parents everywhere, that not all toddler tantrums are tragedies, and that it's okay to laugh at the insanity of it all.

I hope you enjoy the book,

Greg Pembroke
[(reasonsmysoniscrying@gmail.com)](reasonsmysoniscrying@gmail.com)

"Last Father's Day, my three-year-old son rushed excitedly into my room to wake me up. His beaming face was a wonderful thing to see when I opened my eyes. I scooped him up and hugged him as he put his face right up to mine and excitedly screamed,

'Happy Father's Day, Daddy!'

I opened my mouth to thank him, but as I started to speak he made the worst face imaginable and interrupted me – 'Your breath smells YUCKY!'

When I made the decision to work part-time and spend more hours at home with my boys, I admit that I had been all big talk – totally confident that I'd be fine in my new stay-at-home role. But this charming Father's Day story reminds me of that moment when my wife first drove off to work, leaving me home with two boys under two.

For the first time, I learned the true meaning of the word fear…"

'Buzz Lightyear's knee is bent.'

'He asked me to put butter on his rice.
I put butter on his rice.'

'He saw a beetle.'

'His brother pretended to sing for one second.'

'I put the wrong jam on his sandwich.'

'I washed the sand and dirt off his pear.'

'I wouldn't let him drown in this pond.'

'I wouldn't let him get a tattoo.'

'We gave him some delicious pudding.'

'We suggested he play with a train.'

'I told him he couldn't run until they say "go".'

'He took his shoes and socks off.
His feet are now cold.'

'The slide is not slippery enough.'

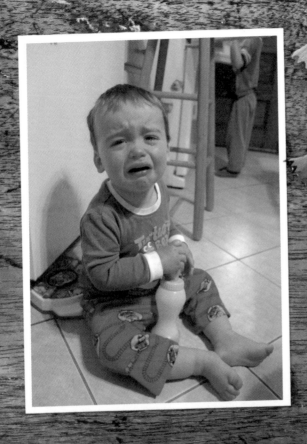

'The neighbor's dog isn't outside.'

Great Expectations

" The great thing about kids is that because they know so little of the world, everything is new and exciting to them. Recently my son and I were having a great time wrestling on the floor, laughing and giggling – a perfect father–son moment.

That is, until he started staring at my hands. I guess he had never noticed my knuckles before. He hated the look of that weird, wrinkly, bunched-up skin – and started tugging on it, demanding that I 'take it off'. When I explained that it just wasn't possible for me to rip my own knuckles off, our fun-filled afternoon wrestlefest turned into the eighth sobbing fit of the day.

Like tiny Bond villains with very small and insanely specific goals, toddlers have great expectations for what life will bring on any given day. Disappoint them at your peril."

'His aunt wouldn't let him play with an ax.'

'He wanted to eat more dirt.'

'We wouldn't let him eat his dad's phone.'

'We wouldn't let him drag his new bookshelf
into the living room.'

'He didn't want to share his leg hole.'

'He threw his blanket on the floor.'

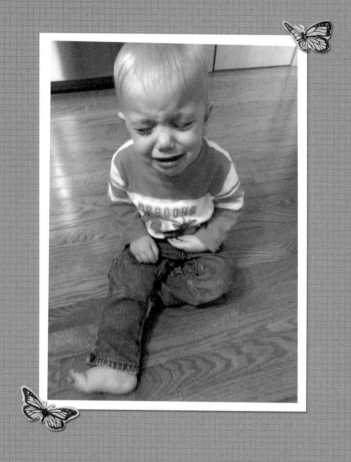

'I wouldn't let him crawl into a 400-degree oven.'

'We turned on his favorite show the
minute he asked us to.'

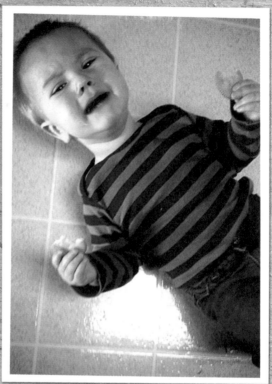

'I thought that since he already had a Ritz cracker in each hand, I could eat one myself without upsetting him.'

'We put together his new balance bike.'

'I asked her to please stop licking
the bottom of her shoe.'

'The remote-controlled car he was driving drove away.'

'It wasn't raining inside.'

'The wind wasn't windy.'

'His train derailed.'

'She decided to go swimming
in the dog's water bowl.'

" One of the joys of parenthood is the passing of wisdom between the generations; the gentle flow of conversation between parent and child. Recently, I tried to teach my three-year-old a joke while we were driving:

'Why did the chicken cross the road?'

'I didn't see any chickens.'

'No, I didn't either, but just SAY there was a chicken who was crossing the road . . .'

'[Concerned] We would hit him with our car!'

'No, okay, what if there was a chicken who wanted to cross the road and there were no cars coming?'

'He would FLY. Can chickens fly, Daddy?'

'Well, no. Hmmm. Maybe, for short distances? I'm actually not sure—'

'LOOK DAD . . . A HORSIE!'

It's a work in progress."

'I told him that he had to hold my hand during
the walk home from daycare.'

'I said I wouldn't give him any more books.'

'I asked him if he wanted to say hi
to Mommy on the phone.'

'I asked him what he wanted for dinner.'

'We told him he had to walk back to the car.'

'He wanted to ride in Daddy's jeep.
NOTE: He was already in Daddy's jeep.'

'We asked him if he was ready
to go get ice cream.'

'We told him he looked very handsome.'

'He couldn't carry the breakfast up
to Daddy on Father's Day.'

'His Skype chat with Grandma
and Grandpa froze.'

'His teacher said "no" . . . to someone else.'

'She bit my finger. I said "Ouch".'

" Parents know that nutritious, home-made meals are necessary to make sure that their kids grow up healthy and strong. Toddlers know that mealtime is a broccoli-filled Thunderdome where only the strongest, smartest and fastest will survive.

When they're very young, you can try the 'spread and spackle' approach – smearing mushy goodness on their face in the hope that some of it makes it past their clenched lips. But as they age, the baffling logic of the hungry toddler, honed through countless millennia of evolution, begins to take over: bread crusts are inedible, and the only acceptable sandwich shape is 'triangle cut'. T-Rex shaped chicken nuggets taste better than Triceratops. And all food is better with ketchup.

Three square meals a day. Three opportunities for total meltdown – many times, ironically, over tuna melts.

'I wouldn't let him drink whiskey.'

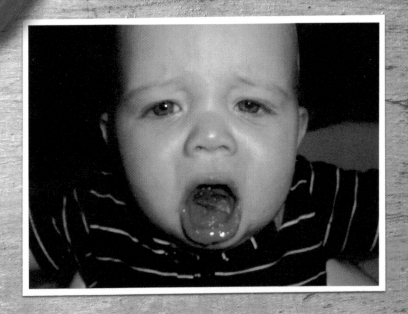

'We thought he might like to try peas.'

'I wouldn't put salt on her apricots.'

'He ate his peach, then got mad that
his peach was gone.'

'A fly landed near him.'

'He ate the last piece of pizza.'

'The banana is over.'

'I told him to stop stuffing
his supper down his pants.'

'His instant oatmeal was not, in fact, instant.'

'She wanted to squeeze her
favorite veggie pouch.'

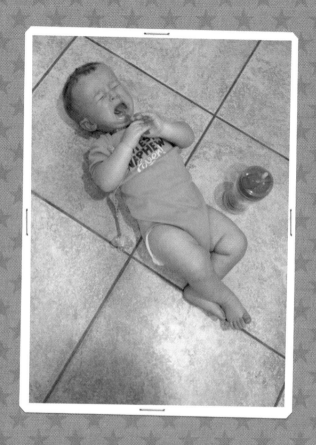

'I gave him peanut butter on a spoon
instead of on my finger.'

'We had to put the cupcakes we were
making into the oven to bake.'

'Her popsicle was cold.'

'He decided to rub mashed potatoes
in his eyes.'

'I told her that I had to wash her
face after dinner.'

'It's just dinner time. Times two.'

" Siblings are the best friends we never asked for. It's no wonder that the source of the greatest joy and pain in the lives of toddlers comes from the people on the planet that they are genetically closest to. They share toys, parents – and sometimes even their faces.

Like most parents, we have extolled the healing virtue of kisses for all manner of injuries over the years, from bumped heads to scraped knees. The other day, I heard my older boy crying. I ran into their bedroom to see his little brother hitting him in the head, and then immediately kissing it to make it 'all better'... and then hitting him again. After turning my head so they couldn't see me laughing, I tried my best to explain that it didn't quite work like that..."

'He threw his dinner on the floor
and now he wants to eat it.'

'We told her that she was going
to have a baby brother.'

'He met his brother for the first time.'

'Her brother sat down.'

'One doesn't want to wear a bib.
One wants to wear the other's bib.'

'I thought we could take a cute
"Big Brother–Little Brother" picture.'

'They got caught between the speaker
and the couch.'

'His sister blocked his kick.'

'It was her turn to steer.'

'Her big sister wanted to take
a picture with her.'

" One of my wife's biggest complaints about having boys is that there just aren't as many 'cute' clothes for them as there are for girls. But she perseveres, scouring stores in search of outfits that will make our boys look like the most handsome prep-school gentlemen you've ever seen.

Those outfits are pristine, unworn and hanging in the closet.

And in their place? Pajamas. At all times. We secretly hope that, when our boys grow up and perhaps get married, they'll be wearing beautifully cut suits, dazzlingly shined shoes and elegant ties. But the smart money is on Buzz Lightyear pajamas with rocket wings."

'We thought he'd like this monkey outfit.'

'I made him this fancy bib.'

'She wanted to dress up like a princess.'

'His sock wouldn't come off.'

'He tried on his new glasses.'

'He wanted underwear on his head.'

'He didn't like any of the 46 pairs of swim
trunks I offered him.'

'I wouldn't let him outside in Daddy's shoes.'

'She took her sandal off, then she couldn't
put it back on.'

'We asked him to try on his costume,
just to make sure it fit.'

66 The toddler birthday: the Olympics of parenting. The day where you show the world – your family, pre-school acquaintances and your 400 closest Facebook friends – once and for all just how much you love your kids, by throwing them the grandest festival since the bacchanals of ancient Greece.

You've bought the balloons, wrapped the presents, rented the bounce houses, hired the clowns, saddled up the miniature ponies, donned the party hats and spread out an array of elaborate cakes and gifts, all sure to delight any child. Yes, you have all the makings of a perfect day ... "

'We thought that this would
make a nice photograph.'

'I wouldn't let him touch the fire.'

'It was his birthday.'

'I tried to feed him birthday cake.'

'We asked her to smash this cake.
She declined.'

'He didn't want to smile for another photo.'

'He ate delicious cake for the first time.'

'We bought him this expensive
barking dog guitar.'

'I wouldn't let him put his hands
in his brother's cake.'

'I took the glass of red wine away from her.'

'We threw him a party and invited
all our friends.'

'There were no more birthday
presents to open.'

" Almost as important as sleep and good nutrition, time spent outdoors is a critical component of toddler happiness. It's also much harder for them to ruin your furniture, gouge your walls, and smash your electronics if they're not at home. A typical trip to the playground for these energetic explorers can include any one of the following time-honored toddler activities:

- Crying because I made them go to the playground
- Crying because there are no other children there
- Crying because there are too many other children there
- Crying because the laws of physics won't allow the swing to go any higher
- Crying because I won't let them chew old gum they found on a bench
- Crying because they had sand thrown at them
- Crying because I won't let them throw sand
- Crying because it's time to go home"

'He doesn't like the grass.'

'We took a relaxing trip to the beach.'

'We couldn't take the lions home with us.'

'The goat got a little too close.'

'The officers let him sit on this motorcycle.'

'His uncle pushed him.'

'We took him to the beach.'

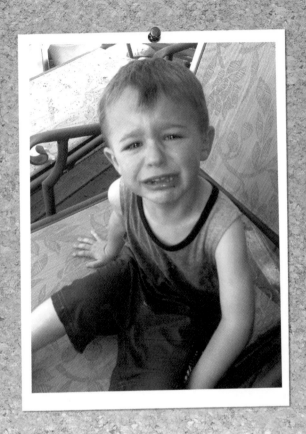

'I wouldn't let him play with the dead
squirrel he found in the yard.'

'We wouldn't let him throw his dad's
glasses down into this lighthouse.'

'We showed him a bonsai tree.'

'He couldn't play in Old Faithful.'

'We took her on her very first bike ride.'

'Water got on his bathing suit.'

**'I took the rocks she was eating
out of her mouth.'**

" Before we had children, we pictured quiet afternoons lounging with our little angels in a bed flowing with soft white linen. We'd laugh, maybe play games in the sunshine and push our kids on an old rope swing near a lazy river.

A few months ago, like a scene from that perfect daydream of family life, I sat my son down, looked him in the eye and told him just how much I loved him. He stared right back at me and told me that, no, I didn't love him. I loved his brother, because HE loved MOMMY. I replied patiently that I loved him, his brother AND Mommy. Again, no – only HE could love Mommy. I tried a few more times to get him to understand the idea of loving everyone in your family equally, but he did some very simple math and quickly decided that Mommy > Daddy. Every single time."

'She didn't want to sit next to her uncle.'

'I went to the mailbox, located one foot
away from the front door.'

'She didn't want to share the pool with Nana.'

'The dog was in the way while he was
trying to push the chair.'

'I pretended my hand was a phone.'

'I let go of his hand to show his grandma
how well he could walk.'

'We wanted to take a father–daughter photo
to remember this beautiful day.'

'The modem stopped flashing.'

'I wouldn't ride with her. (I am 6' 4",
it's not physically possible.)

'I put the toy bull on the second level
of the barn instead of ground level.'

'We thought it would be fun to take
him to the pool.'

'I wouldn't let him electrocute himself.'

'The dog would not sit still long
enough for him to eat her tail.'

'We told her she had to take Grandma's glasses off so that she could see.'

'He put himself in "time-out"
for no reason.'

'I wouldn't let him climb into
the dishwasher.'

THE END OF A PERFECT DAY

HAIR AND BODY WASH FOR SENSITIVE SKIN

"After a full day of living, laughing and loving, toddlers are happy and excited about bath time. There is nothing they love more than sitting still while you lovingly wash and rinse their hair. Or that's how I once imagined bath time would be. In reality they splash at least six liters of water on the floor and fight like cats over their toys, while I am forced to shout phrases I never thought I'd need: 'Do NOT sit on your brother's head!', and 'STOP PEEING ON YOUR BROTHER'.

Johnson & Johnson offer a 'No More Tears' formula for their baby shampoo. I want an adult version."

'We stopped him from eating this
roll of toilet paper.'

'I wouldn't let her eat the glow stick.'

'The diaper is gone.'

'He threw his toys into the toilet.'

'I wouldn't let him finish eating
the diaper cream.'

'Daddy didn't want a bathroom audience.'

'Her dad is stuck in the computer.'

'I wouldn't let him sleep in the
bathtub overnight.'

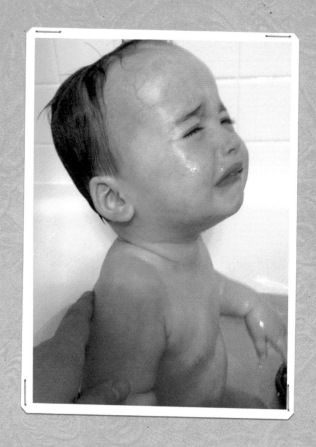

'I wouldn't let him drink bathwater.'

'I read him his favorite bedtime story.'

'I have no idea why my son is crying.'

" I would like to offer my sincerest thanks to the thousands of families that submitted photos for this book and for my website. It's a truly remarkable community that we have established. It's so refreshing to find these common pieces of human ground in a world that grows ever more divided.

And of course, I would be utterly remiss not to also thank my beautiful crying boys. I know we choose to celebrate some of the silly reasons for your tears, but always remember that the laughter and joy you both bring washes away any sadness, tenfold. The last four years have been an incredible journey and I cannot wait to relish the adventures, hilarity (and mischief) that await us all as a family in the future!"